Portraits

A MONTH IN THE LIFE OF THE SALVATION ARMY
IN THE UNITED KINGDOM TERRITORY
WITH THE REPUBLIC OF IRELAND

Portraits

A MONTH IN THE LIFE OF THE SALVATION ARMY
IN THE UNITED KINGDOM TERRITORY
WITH THE REPUBLIC OF IRELAND

Acknowledgements
Thank you to everyone involved in the production of *Portraits: A Month in the Life of The Salvation Army* and to those who supported the project:

Commissioners John and Betty Matear, territorial leaders, and senior leadership of the United Kingdom Territory with the Republic of Ireland
Major Leanne Ruthven, Editor-in-Chief and Publishing Secretary, and members of the Territorial Literary Council
Cathy Le Feuvre, Project Manager
Paul Harmer, photography
Photograph of Her Majesty The Queen by John Swannell, Camera Press, London
Robert Gould, design

Thank you also to everyone who submitted photographs, notes and quotes for this book. Hundreds of submissions were received from Salvation Army corps, social centres, headquarters departments and individuals. There are too many contributors to mention individually but, whether your photos are included in this book or not, we are grateful for your contributions.

And finally, thanks to God — may he continue to use The Salvation Army for his glory.

Published by The Salvation Army
United Kingdom Territory with the Republic of Ireland
101 Newington Causeway, London SE1 6BN

Contents

Her Majesty The Queen

IT IS with great pleasure that, in this year of my Diamond Jubilee, I send my best wishes to The Salvation Army in the United Kingdom and the Republic of Ireland as it celebrates its 2012 Congress in London.

In the century since the Army's Founder, General William Booth, delivered his final address at the Royal Albert Hall, this Christian organisation has inspired and supported millions of people around the world. The message of God's love for all is as relevant in the 21st century as it was one hundred years ago, and this book is a testament to The Salvation Army's continuing ministry.

I congratulate those who have participated in the project and have no doubt that the images in this book will inspire not only members and friends of The Salvation Army, but every one of us.

Elizabeth R
February, 2012

General Linda Bond

PORTRAITS: A Month in the Life of The Salvation Army is so much more than a souvenir book, though it is also that. It tells a story. It captures the essence of who we are by showing what we do.

It has always been the conviction of Salvationists that our faith must be expressed in words and actions. The Salvation Army in the United Kingdom and the Republic of Ireland is living up to the vision of its Founder, William Booth. But even more significantly, as followers of Jesus Christ, Salvationists follow his example of meeting human need, reaching out to the marginalised in compassionate and creative ways.

General Linda Bond
International Leader of The Salvation Army

Foreword

THE Salvation Army is known for its innovative ways of sharing the good news of Jesus Christ. We aim to be an outward-looking people, ready to try anything for the sake of those who have not yet heard the gospel.

This book captures some of the ways Salvationists are doing just that, 100 years after the death of the Army's founder, William Booth. We worship God inside and outside our church buildings, and we meet people wherever they are and whatever their need.

This book is called *Portraits* because people are our focus. We believe every person, without exception, is made in the image of God and loved deeply by him. This book provides a 'snapshot' over a calendar month of how The Salvation Army in the United Kingdom and the Republic of Ireland demonstrates that belief.

The 21st-century Army may look different to the organisation William Booth and his wife Catherine founded in the late 1800s, yet the reason for our existence has not changed. God has raised us up to worship him and to serve the 'least, last and lost' of society. We are determined to continue to worship God with our whole being, and to fight for justice for those who cannot speak for themselves.

From the youngest members of our parent-and-toddler groups to the senior citizens in our corps; from stories of changed lives in our Lifehouse centres to a quiet moment with an older person living with dementia; and from the images of Salvation Army brass bands to more private moments of our Christian worship – I trust this book will not just capture your interest, but challenge and inspire you.

'For we do not preach ourselves, but Jesus Christ as Lord, and ourselves as your servants for Jesus' sake,' wrote the apostle Paul in 2 Corinthians chapter 4, verse 5 (*New International Version*).

This is our motivation.

God bless you.

John Matear, Commissioner
Territorial Commander 2006 – 2012
United Kingdom Territory with the Republic of Ireland

Introduction

I N May 1912, General William Booth, Founder of The Salvation Army, stood for the final time in the Royal Albert Hall in London. Approaching the end of his life, and virtually blind, he still possessed a vibrant, fighting spirit.

With his wife Catherine, William Booth had spent a lifetime creating a Christian 'movement' which was both a church and a charity – at the heart of which was a love for God and people of all ages, classes, races and social circumstances.

From its meagre beginnings in the East End of London in 1865, The Salvation Army, which until 1878 was known as The Christian Mission, had by 1912 grown into an international organisation, renowned not just for its Christian beliefs, vibrant worship and outreach, but also for its focus on social mission, social justice and social action.

William Booth believed that through the saving grace of God, the acceptance of Jesus Christ as Saviour and by the power of the Holy Spirit, the world could be changed for the better. As he came to the end of his life – he was 'promoted to Glory' on 20 August 1912 – Booth was determined to leave his thousands of 'soldiers' (who had become known as Salvationists) with a resounding challenge: to put all their efforts into fighting sin and making the world a better place.

In 2012 – a century on from the Founder's final speech – The Salvation Army is still pointing people to faith in Jesus Christ, fighting for social justice and reaching out to those in need. In more than 120 countries across the world William Booth's vision continues to flourish.

To mark the May 2012 centenary of the Royal Albert Hall speech, Salvation Army corps (churches) and centres across the United Kingdom and Republic of Ireland were invited to submit photographs and stories that demonstrate the continuing work of this unique organisation. As such, this is a record of the Army's ministry through the eyes of those who contributed. All the photographs in this book, which include some professional images, were taken across one calendar month – October 2011.

However, this book is not just for Salvationists, but for anyone interested in this group of people who make a difference to society. It is about the work God is doing in and through the people associated with it – members, friends, employees, service-users – whether they are pictured here or not.

As William Booth wrote in an autograph album in October 1910: 'Your days at the most cannot be very long, so use them to the best of your ability for the glory of God and the benefit of your generation.'

THE Salvation Army is a church. For those who know it only as a provider of social services, this may come as a surprise. First and foremost, the Army is a Christian (Protestant) denomination and its motivation for worship and social action comes directly from its faith.

The Army's Founder, William Booth, didn't originally set out to form a new church; his mission was to see people become Christians and then link up with an established church. However, it wasn't long before new Salvation Army congregations (corps) sprang up. It's because of this history that the Army still describes itself as a Christian 'movement' as well as a church.

Today Salvation Army corps vary in size and character, but everywhere the focus is the same: to worship God and serve others in his name.

Praise

'We are a salvation people. Let us seek first the Kingdom of God'

William Booth

RIGHT
Captain Ian Woodgate preaches to his Sunday congregation at Horsham.

Worship

HORSHAM is a multigenerational corps in West Sussex where everyone is welcome and life is busy. Through a range of activities, from worship and Bible study to craft clubs and prayer ministry, the corps makes contact with up to 500 people each week.

Captains Ian and Susan Woodgate lead the corps in Horsham.

'The heart of our worship meetings is simply that Jesus Christ will be glorified and lifted high,' says Ian. 'We seek to embrace every generation and provide a relevant and vibrant ministry in the name of Jesus. Our vision is to bring "Hope for Today", and this is the foundation for all our activities.'

'Where the name of Jesus Christ is lifted high, people will be drawn to him'

Captain Ian Woodgate

'Place of Hope,
people of Hope,
proclamation of
Hope and promise
of Hope'
Horsham Salvation Army
Mission Statement

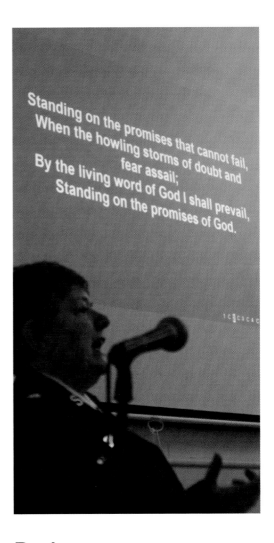

Maidstone

There's a warm Sunday welcome to lively, thoughtful, all-age worship at The Salvation Army in Maidstone, with congregational singing, participation from junior and senior music groups and biblical teaching.

Praise

Praising the Lord at Newbury, Clevedon and Stowmarket.

Prayer

PRAYER is a vital part of Christianity and is central to Salvation Army life.

It is always a part of worship and traditionally congregation members have been encouraged to pray out loud during services.

Private, public and corporate prayer is encouraged from a young age and is woven into all aspects of Army life, including lunch clubs, music rehearsals and staff meetings.

Along with study of the Bible, The Salvation Army believes that talking with God and listening to him are essential for a healthy Christian life.

'You must pray with all your might'

William Booth

The Salvation Army for a new generation

ALOVE, The Salvation Army's youth department, works with teenagers through to young adults. As well as local events and activities there are annual rallies. In October 2011 Territorial Youth Secretaries Majors Andrea and Mark Sawyer took their Youth Rally on Tour around the country. It was enjoyed by thousands of young Salvationists and friends.

'We at ALOVE continue to call young people to a life of dynamic faith, radical living, adventurous mission and fighting for justice'

Major Mark Sawyer

Youth Rally on Tour

Youth worship

Culturally relevant worship is vital to the development of young Christians, who enjoyed DJ-led praise during Youth Rally on Tour. Majors Mark and Andrea Sawyer (right) preached.

West Midlands Youth Day

A fun day of lively worship took place at the West Midlands regional youth rally. Delegates rehearsed and later performed music and a 'Stomp' routine featuring old saucepans, rubbish bins and much more.

ALOVE trains future leaders and youth workers through its Essential programmes. The Gap Year students work in Salvation Army corps and centres and meet for training days.

Honing skills

Renowned Christian worship leader Geraldine Latty, who has been a guest at many Salvation Army events, leads vibrant praise as part of an East Midlands worship seminar.

Young people in worship

THE Salvation Army believes even young people can have an understanding of God and faith. Children can become junior soldiers (members) at the age of seven, and are often directly involved in meetings – taking part in music groups, Bible reading and praying. Many corps provide activities specifically for children.

Kettering Corps
At Kettering in Northamptonshire, the singing company practises hard every week.

Staple Hill

The first Sunday of every month at Staple Hill Corps in Bristol is a relaxed 'Good Morning Sunday' and October's theme was teamwork and the Rugby World Cup. Sport lovers Luke, Adam and Josh, who play for the corps football team, had the challenge of beating the corps officer in a rugby scrum.

Birmingham Citadel

At Birmingham Citadel the children take part in the weekly Sunday services – here they are helping out with a story. The junior music groups practise every week and then take part in Sunday meetings.

Coventry City

Salvation Army corps with children usually hold a Young People's Anniversary Weekend where the focus is completely on the children. At Coventry City the very youngest (primary) children took part in the service, the junior music sections participated and young people also led prayers.

Nottingham

In October 2011 the Young People's Band at William Booth Memorial Halls in Nottingham celebrated 100 years. It was a special day for Phillip Clarke who was commissioned as the newest band member that day and got to cut the birthday cake with Peter Cooke, a former band member, and the band leader Kevin Pallister.

Scarborough

Scarborough in Yorkshire held a celebration where the children took part.

Worship bands

MUSIC plays an important part in Salvation Army services, which are traditionally held on Sundays, but can also take place at other times.

Many corps have brass bands whose primary role is to accompany worship, while some have groups with guitars, keyboards and percussion. This is not a 21st-century phenomenon – the Army has even had pop groups, the most popular of these being the Joystrings, which had several chart hits in the 1960s.

Corps often have songster brigades (choirs) as well, along with bands and singing companies for young people.

Musically, diversity is the key at the Army.

Leading the way

Breakthru sings at Birmingham Citadel (below); worship time at Aberdeen Citadel (right); and Romford Worship Group leads worship during a Sunday morning service (below right).

International Staff Band
and
International Staff Songsters

THE International Staff Band and International Staff Songsters are the premier brass band and choir in The Salvation Army. These groups were created to bring excellence and inspiration to music-making, with their primary purpose being Christian ministry and outreach.

They take part in large Army events such as Christmas with The Salvation Army at the Royal Albert Hall, make media appearances and record music. Both groups have toured extensively overseas, but their priority is the visits to corps and communities around the UK and Republic of Ireland.

Membership in these groups is a heavy commitment; many of them are leaders in their own corps and, like many Army musicians, juggle work and family responsibilities.

International Staff Band

In October 2011 the band, under conductor Dr Stephen Cobb, visited Stowmarket Salvation Army in Suffolk. They presented a concert at the Ipswich Corn Exchange (above) and led Sunday worship at the corps, where local music sections (below) also took part.

The weekend was part of Stowmarket's 125th anniversary celebrations. During Sunday meetings band members not only presented music, but also spoke about their Christian faith.

In June 2011 the band celebrated its 120th anniversary with a weekend of spectacular events that featured eight other Salvation Army staff bands from around the world.

Activities included a sell-out concert at the Royal Albert Hall and a march down the Mall in London that culminated in the eight bands playing in the forecourt of Buckingham Palace.

International Staff Songsters

Formed in 1980, this group exists to communicate the Christian gospel through music and to encourage people in the Christian faith.

In October 2011, the songsters visited Belfast Sydenham, one of several Salvation Army corps in the Northern Ireland capital. Under their leader Dorothy Nancekievill they performed a Saturday concert at Belmont Presbyterian Church, and on the Sunday led lively worship at Sydenham Corps.

Drama in worship

THE Salvation Army has a history of using dramatic performance to share the gospel message. For many years the Army produced stage musicals, written chiefly by two officers, John Gowans and John Larsson, both of whom went on to become Generals (world leaders of The Salvation Army). Keith Turton, the Territorial Drama Co-ordinator, has the task of promoting drama and performance across the UK and Republic of Ireland.

Dramatic words

Keith Turton and Claire Brine rehearse at Territorial Headquarters in London in advance of a short November 2011 tour of *Dramatic Words* – a collection of pieces relating to Christian themes.

Dramatic kids

In October 2011 Keith spent a week in Maidstone in Kent for the half term Holiday Drama Week. Thirty children aged 6 to 12, most of whom had no previous contact with The Salvation Army, attended for more than two hours a day, learning songs and lines and dance routines. The week ended with an energetic one-off performance.

'I hadn't expected it to be so well done'

A happy Maidstone parent

Dramatic worship

Clevedon Corps drama group The King's Messengers rehearse.

Messy Church
A different approach

'God is blessing this
ministry and challenging
us to widen our vision'

Major Neil Davies, Bridgwater, Somerset

ANY people in the UK no longer have the 'church-going habit' so The Salvation Army is always looking for new ways to attract people to its activities.

Messy Church happens in many corps, including Bridgwater, Luton, Ripley and Leicester South. Here people of all ages can explore faith and worship through celebration, craft work – and food! It's about helping people see that church can be inclusive and enjoyable, as well as beneficial for their spiritual life.

'It's a big team effort but worth the huge investment'

Carolyn Gomersall, Children and Families Worker,
Luton Salvation Army

35

INCE its beginnings in the East End of London The Salvation Army has been committed to people; in particular, raising awareness about human trafficking and assisting its victims has always been important. As early as 1882 Catherine Booth, the 'Army Mother', wrote about the organisation's commitment to rescuing women held in captivity for the purpose of sexual exploitation.

In 2011 The Salvation Army became responsible for the UK government contract to manage the support provided to victims of human trafficking across England and Wales. Working with experienced partners and providers, the Army manages the delivery of accommodation and support for male and female victims of all kinds of trafficking, including sexual exploitation, domestic servitude and forced labour.

People

'While women weep, as they do now, I'll fight'

William Booth

RIGHT
Major Anne Read is The Salvation Army's Anti-Human Trafficking Response Co-ordinator and part of the team managing the government contract. In October 2011 Major Read represented The Salvation Army at an anti-slavery event at the House of Lords.

I N addition to the national anti-trafficking contract, Salvation Army corps are also becoming increasingly involved in assisting people who find themselves the victims of trafficking.

Most centres that do so work in coalition with other groups. Chelmsford Corps, for example, held a fundraising event in October 2011 to support the work.

'Victims of human trafficking are treated as "things" to be bought and sold, with no value whatsoever except for the money that can be made from their sale. Trafficking is modern-day slavery! The Bible teaches that every human being is immensely valuable in the sight of God: "You have made them a little lower than the angels and crowned them with glory and honour" (Psalm 8, verse 5).

'The moment a trafficked person comes into the care of The Salvation Army we aim to ensure they feel loved and valued as we show them unconditional Christian compassion and kindness. And that's just the start of a journey of renewal, as they rediscover their value and worth as part of God's creation.'

Major Anne Read
Anti-Human Trafficking Response Co-ordinator

Chelmsford Corps members take part in the quiz night.

'To mark Anti-Slavery Day 2011, members of Chelmsford Corps who are involved with the town's Active Community Against Trafficking group helped arrange a quiz night. The evening was attended by 75 people and each round included a bonus question relating to human trafficking so that awareness could be raised regarding the issue'

Major Derek Jones, Chelmsford

Anti-trafficking education

To put an end to this modern slave trade, prevention is vital. In Qinghai province in north-west China, The Salvation Army works with communities where people are at risk of being trafficked. The work is funded by the Army in the UK, Australia and Sweden and representatives visited in October 2011 to see how the projects were progressing.

Putting people first

WHEN William Booth saw the plight of homeless people living on the streets of London, he recognised that part of The Salvation Army's mission should be to help people in desperate circumstances. He urged his son, Bramwell, to do something in response to the need all around them. Helping people improve their situation, move on with their lives and find new purpose – that's what The Salvation Army is still all about.

'Go and do something!'
William Booth

Inspiring

THE EVA Burrows 1st Stop Project in Cambuslang in Scotland provides housing for families and individuals awaiting rehousing by the local council.

In October 2011 a group of residents and staff took part in their first ever hill walking activity to Conic Hill. The steep 3km walk, which is part of the West Highland Way, runs between Balmaha, at the meeting place between the Scottish Highlands and Lowlands, and Loch Lomond.

'The activity had a positive impact on everyone who took part – staff and service users – in particular promoting physical health and the development of relationships.'
Helen McKay, Centre Manager, Eva Burrows 1st Stop Project

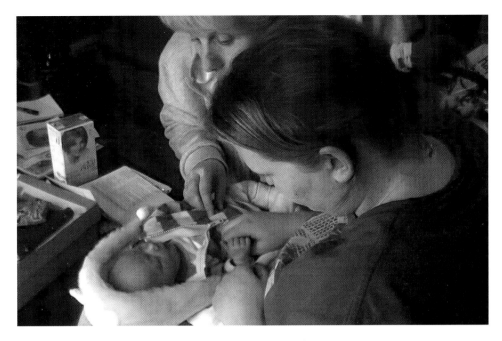

Shield Project, Aberdeenshire

A young mum, at risk of having to put her child into care, was allowed to take her baby home thanks to the support of The Salvation Army Shield Project in Peterhead. This project works with people who are homeless or at risk of becoming so, with rough sleepers and with those in temporary accommodation, many of whom are struggling with substance abuse.

The aim is to keep people in accommodation while assisting them to quit drugs or alcohol, and to help them seek spiritual wholeness. Local churches donate food, while financial counselling, basic life skills training, medical care and even support for court appearances are offered. The staff work with 57 people – and there's a waiting list.

Logos House Bristol

At this supported housing centre, service users are encouraged to develop skills and take up healthy activities. Indian Head Massage is one of the therapies offered as it can help with anxiety and sleeping difficulties. Sport is also an important part of rehabilitation.

Helping people on the streets

Friends and volunteers from Winton Salvation Army are part of the churches' outreach in the seaside town of Bournemouth which offers meal runs for street people. Mary Randell, MBE, co-ordinates the project.

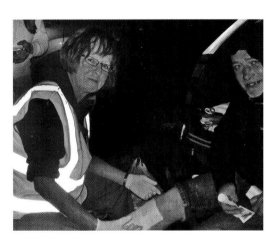

Right: Nurse Rosemarie Veale offers treatment – feet and legs are often badly affected when people live on the streets.

'Every Monday evening on our Winton meal run we have an open-air clinic. Some of the poorest people in our town come for free treatment. Not one of our team would ever judge these precious people, they are our friends, and I am certain that if Jesus were here now he would be reaching out to them.'
Mary Randell

Worthing

More than 130 people are part of the Thursday Club at Worthing Salvation Army. This group supports people aged 15 to 30 who have special needs – from learning and behavioural difficulties to epilepsy, Down's syndrome and spina bifida.

Between 70 and 100 people attend each week, having been referred by social workers, carers, parents or teachers. This club is the only evening programme in the area that provides a supervised environment for people with special needs. Here they enjoy some dancing.

The Welcome Break, held on Thursday mornings, provides carers with rest and support while those they look after enjoy separate activities (below). Many carers and clients then choose to stay for lunch at the Army's community centre, the Welcome In.

Peterborough

At Peterborough Citadel Day Centre (above and facing page) people of all ages get together, learn new skills, enjoy a meal, have fun and receive support.

Volunteers from the Good Neighbours Scheme befriend those who might otherwise become isolated. Older people are helped so they can remain in their own homes for as long as possible, and there's even a free gardening service.

Peterborough Citadel is one of several corps that run debt centres for people needing financial guidance and support. Increasingly important as Britain experiences economic downturn, Salvation Army debt centres are places where people can be made aware of other groups and agencies who may be able to help.

Community Opportunities, Leicester South

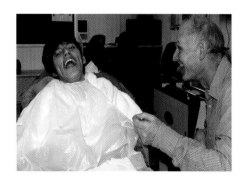

Leicester South hosts a Community Opportunities Group three days a week for recreation and occupational therapy, working in co-operation with South Leicester Day Services.

A time for everything

In common with other churches, the Army provides support from 'cradle to grave'. People of all ages are welcome

Dedication

In The Salvation Army children are 'dedicated to God' rather than christened, and at Birmingham Citadel Mollie Poppy Lamplough's parents brought her to be dedicated.

Dad Gavin, who is the corps bandmaster, and mum Stephanie, who leads the singing company (junior choir), promised during the ceremony to raise Mollie in the Christian faith. They prayed that she will eventually embrace the faith for herself. Salvationists believe that you don't inherit Christianity, but that each person must come to faith for themselves.

The dedication service is a public event that often takes place during the Sunday morning service.

Promotion to Glory

Funerals in The Salvation Army are a time for reflection but also rejoicing as we believe death for the Christian means they are with God, in heaven. That's why Salvationists are 'promoted to Glory'. The Army flag, trimmed with white ribbon, stands in honour of the one who has died.

In October, the Army in Reading Central celebrated the life and service of Molly Tickner.

Weddings

The Army believes in family life and is committed to supporting families whatever form they take and to celebrate with them on special occasions.

Deputy Bandmaster Trevor and Songster Sheila James (above) celebrated their Golden Wedding Anniversary at Clevedon Corps in October 2011.

At Stowmarket Francis and Patricia Leeks (right) celebrated 60 years of marriage. Corps officer Major Dianne Henderson led a special service.

Some people choose to celebrate their marriage in The Salvation Army and one October Sunday morning at Horsham, Les and Marion Daniels (above) celebrated their Wedding Blessing surrounded by family and church friends.

'Mum had a fascinating life. She was fostered as a baby from The Salvation Army's Cotland Mother and Baby Home in East London and this resulted in a lifetime of love and service in the Army.

'Just before the funeral, we showed pictures of Mum's life including one of Mum and Dad in their courting days before the war – Mum in her bonnet! Mum was a Sunday school leader and one of her "girls", Major Christine Bailey, conducted the funeral.'

Major Rachel Tickner,
Molly's daughter

Investing in people

THE Salvation Army in the UK and Republic of Ireland involves thousands of people. There are nearly 30,000 church members of all ages led by around 1,200 officers – ordained ministers of religion.

Many more are reached through its social services networks: 'Lifehouses' (accommodation-based supported housing), older people's centres and community centres. The Army also employs thousands of staff who come from diverse cultural, faith and economic backgrounds.

Professional training and support for staff is vital at all levels, from the work of the national Human Resources Department to local and regional training days.

In October 2011 the East Midlands Division held a men's training day.

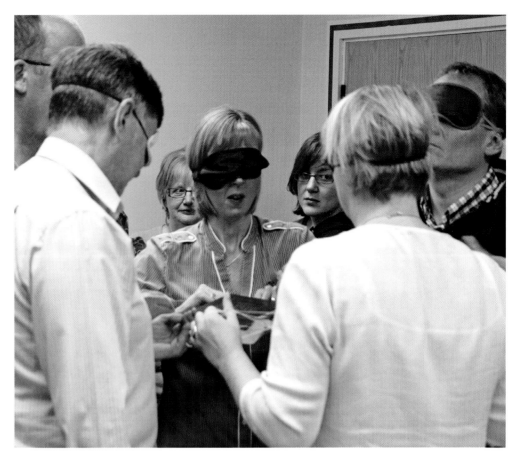

Training

Training children's leaders in the Ireland Division (top) and the busy Human Resources Department at Territorial Headquarters in London (right and below).

(Above and below)
Fun and laughter during a Central North Divisional Headquarters staff training day held in Sale, Manchester.

Strategy and support

Personal and work-related support, training and resources for staff are a vital investment for The Salvation Army as a church, charity and social welfare provider

Team meetings

At Central North Divisional Headquarters, as at all levels of Salvation Army professional life, regular strategy and team meetings are held. Divisional leaders Majors Melvyn and Kathleen Jones (left) discuss a strategic issue relating to their 'patch' with team members, and (above) enjoy a moment of relaxation during the weekly team meeting in Manchester.

Safeguarding

The Army's robust Safeguarding policy protects children and vulnerable adults. Territorial Safeguarding Officer Dean Juster (right) delivers training and supports staff across the country.

Ian Hammond (below), Director of The Salvation Army's HR Employee Unit, shares a confidential 'one-to-one' with a colleague.

Strategic Information

Martyn Croft, the Army's Chief Information Officer, heads up the Strategic Information (SI) Department at Territorial Headquarters in London. SI is responsible for the information systems and technology at the core of Army operations — including computer support for its thousands of staff and officers. Highly respected in the sector, Martyn represents The Salvation Army at national and international conferences and in October was a guest speaker at the Citrix Synergy 2011 Conference in Barcelona, Spain.

'Being invited to speak at the conference provided a great opportunity to share with our peers the way The Salvation Army is employing ... technologies to further the mission'

Martyn Croft

Officers Councils

EVERY two years all active Salvation Army officers (ministers) meet for Councils. This is a time of retreat, inspiration and fellowship, when the Army's territorial leaders meet with their personnel. With around 1,200 active officers, five separate three-day sessions are held in order to cater for everyone. For many years these have been held at The Hayes Christian Conference Centre at Swanwick in Derbyshire.

Teaching

Territorial Commander Commissioner John Matear, in his last Councils before retirement, addresses his 'troops'.

Catching up

At Councils officers are able to meet their leaders – here senior territorial leaders greet their people.

Worship

It's a time for worship – both formal and informal – accompanied at this October 2011 session by a worship group consisting of officers from London South East Division.

New members

Delegates are getting younger! Small children accompany their parents.

Friends

Councils are also a time for catching up with old friends and meeting new ones. Some people only meet once every couple of years.

New members

Two new soldiers are welcomed at Hythe

EVERY week The Salvation Army welcomes new members and friends. Soldiers (full members) of the Army are usually enrolled during Sunday services, where they sign a solemn covenant with God. Other people become adherent members, officially associating themselves with The Salvation Army as their church.

Salvation Army corps also commission people to specific roles in the church, such as musicians or group leaders, or to administrative positions.

53

Come and meet each other

C AMEO (Come And Meet Each Other) clubs, predominantly for the over 60s, are held at many corps across the country every week. There are also women's meetings, called Home League, with resources provided by the Adult and Families Ministries Unit in London. Each CAMEO and Home League meeting may be slightly different, depending on the community and the interests of those attending — from special speakers, to games and activities like bowls at Ipswich Citadel.

Regent Hall, London

Romford

Southampton Shirley

Stowmarket

Blackpool Citadel

Together
Ajuan and Guiwang celebrate their marriage with daughter, friends and Salvation Army support workers

Ajuan's story
Helping reunite families

JUAN moved into The Salvation Army's Leeds Mount Cross Families Lifehouse in December 2009, after fleeing China with her fiancé Guiwang and their daughter, Grace. While Ajuan and Grace received permission to stay in the UK until 2014, Guiwang was returned to China and Ajuan found herself in need of a home and support.

Salvation Army project workers at Mount Cross worked closely with Ajuan and the Refugee Integration and Employment Service to access funds to meet her and her daughter's basic needs. After she had moved into permanent council housing, they continued to support her and assisted with applications to the Home Office Immigration Services to enable her fiancé to return to Leeds.

In September 2011 Guiwang was granted legal status to reside in the UK and just a few weeks later, in October, the couple were married at Leeds Town Hall.

Down Mexico way

At Salisbury House Lifehouse in St Helens the occasional themed evenings are a great success. It's a chance for everyone – service users and staff – to enjoy each other's company and sample foods from other countries. October 2011's Mexican Night saw staff dressing accordingly.

Roller-coaster ride

Service users from Witham Lodge in Skegness who had volunteered 50 hours of their time under the HOPE community project visited Alton Towers.

At work and play

EVERYONE needs to have fun, and most Salvation Army corps and centres schedule some form of recreation into their activities. Sometimes this is combined with other purposes – education, fundraising or team bonding. And sometimes it's just fun for fun's sake. Here's how some Lifehouse staff and service users let their hair down.

Fundraising

At Kings Ripton Court, a centre for 16- to 25-year-olds, participants in the One Step Forward Resettlement Course are eager to support worthy causes. In October 2011 service users and staff took part in a Breast Cancer Awareness 'wear pink day'.

Stars in their Eyes

Fun and laughter at the annual 'Stars in their Eyes' concert at Swan Lodge Lifehouse in Sunderland.

Outings

Witham Lodge service users who complete a six-week resettlement course get to choose an educational outing. Some chose The Deep Aquarium in Hull and others the Transport Museum, Hull.

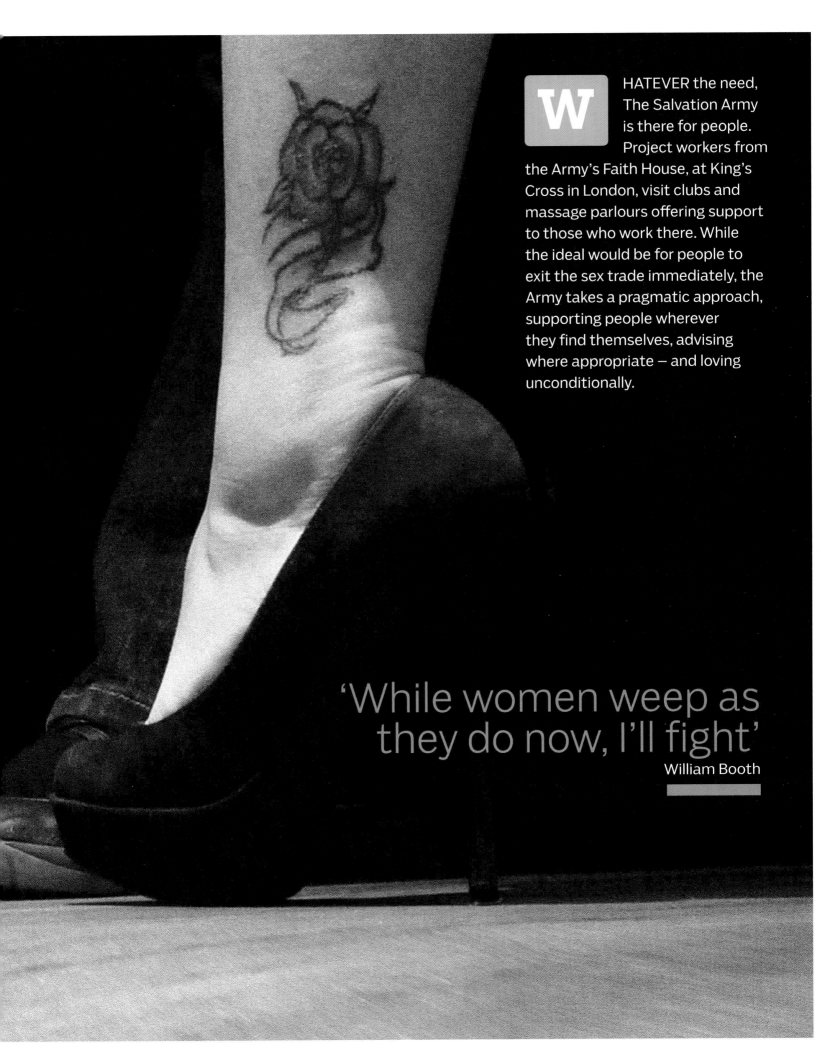

WHATEVER the need, The Salvation Army is there for people. Project workers from the Army's Faith House, at King's Cross in London, visit clubs and massage parlours offering support to those who work there. While the ideal would be for people to exit the sex trade immediately, the Army takes a pragmatic approach, supporting people wherever they find themselves, advising where appropriate – and loving unconditionally.

'While women weep as they do now, I'll fight'

William Booth

THE Salvation Army is to be found in many places. It is international, with a presence in more than 120 countries. It's national – in the UK it is a renowned church and charity, and one of the largest social welfare providers after the Government.

But most people know the Army at the local level: through a drop-in centre, the brass band on the streets or corps-based activities for older people, families, teenagers and young children. Around the nation the Army works tirelessly to support communities, with programmes undertaken by local people who understand their community and its needs.

It has been said: 'Where there's a need, there's The Salvation Army.' Whatever and wherever the need, the Army's motivation remains unchanged from William Booth's day: to share the Christian gospel and reach out to others in a relevant way with love and compassion.

Places

'How wide is the world? We must grow 'til our arms get right round about it!'

William Booth

RIGHT
Graham Wharton is the manager of Southwick Community Project in Sunderland. Graham is also a member of The Salvation Army at nearby Sunderland Monkwearmouth Corps.

Southwick Community Project

At the heart of local life

THE Salvation Army has several corps and centres in Sunderland in the north-east of England. The Southwick Community Project began in 1998 and in 2005 moved into a modern, specially built centre – Austin House Family Centre.

Southwick is ranked among the top five per cent of the UK's most deprived areas and the Army is at its heart, making a positive impact on lives, providing everything from children's activities to support for older people, from food parcels for struggling families to a safe place for teenagers.

Helping older people

Older members of the community need help in getting to and from activities. For many, this might be their only outing of the week.

Lunch

Smiles all round from staff, volunteers and clients during lunch at Southwick Community Project – a lively, vibrant place with a great sense of togetherness.

'I don't just believe God is working in this area, I know he is working here – because I see him every day in this community'

Graham Wharton, manager Southwick Community Project

New places

T HE Salvation Army is still opening new buildings. In October 2011 territorial leaders Commissioners John and Betty Matear visited Newark in the Midlands to open an eco-friendly corps hall. Looking towards a greener future, this is believed to be the first Army centre to produce its own electricity using photovoltaic solar panels. In the first three months of operation the 45 panels on the roof resulted in a £1,300 rebate as the building generated surplus energy that was pumped back into the national grid.

Funding support

Funding for the Newark hall came from various sources including legacies and grants trusts. Nottingham City Councillor Brian Grocock, chair of the Waste Regeneration Environmental Landfill Communities Fund Advisory Panel, presented a plaque to corps officer Major Tim Justice in recognition of its £50,000 grant towards the cost of the new centre.

Bramwell House

In October 2011 Bramwell House Lifehouse in Blackburn reopened its resettlement facility, which was closed after serious flooding in December 2010. Service users affectionately renamed it Phoenix House and the Mayor was one of the guests at the reopening.

Left: Service user Jim Reeves with the Mayor of Blackburn, Councillor Mrs Karimeh Foster, and her consort Councillor David Foster.

Making an impact

In October 2011 work started on an extension to the Impact Centre youth activity and resources building at The Salvation Army in Bourne, Lincolnshire.

The Impact Centre first opened its doors three years ago in the old charity shop behind the hall.

Thanks to a local grants trust and building firm the Impact Centre was completed early in 2012. The Army now has a dedicated youth area and can develop its work with young people in Bourne.

Left: Bourne and District Round Table made a £2,125 donation towards the project. This was received from its chairman by youth worker Vicky Elson.

William Booth College

Training future Salvation Army leaders

I N 1929, as a memorial to the Founder, William Booth College was opened at Denmark Hill in London. It has been at the heart of Salvation Army leadership training ever since and is at the forefront of delivering education and training programmes for the United Kingdom and further afield. The iconic building, designed by Sir Giles Gilbert Scott, still stands but over the first weekend of October 2011 it reopened after extensive refurbishment. The weekend also included the welcome of the newest Salvation Army cadets – officer-trainees – who will spend two years in training for a life of Christian ministry.

The Assembly Hall

The historic Assembly Hall stands at the heart of life at the college. At the front is the 'mercy seat' (above), a focal point of Salvation Army worship that symbolises the central message of salvation that is available to all. The mercy seat is a place where people can pray, publicly declare their Christian faith, or receive counselling.

At any one time there are two sessions of students in residence at William Booth College, with each group having a name that is shared by Salvation Army cadets around the world. In October 2011 the Proclaimers of the Resurrection were welcomed to the college, joining the Friends of Christ, who had just completed their first year of training.

At the back of the Assembly Hall the flags of earlier sessions of cadets are displayed, symbolising the dedication of the thousands trained there in the 83 years of the college's existence.

Left: A Friend of Christ cadet.

The Hub

A new 'Hub' (top) now links two older iconic buildings on the site, the Administration Building and the Assembly Hall.

Right: Proclaimers of the Resurrection cadets.

Family friendly

Many people training for full-time ministry in The Salvation Army come to college with their families – the crèche (left) and the playground have also had a facelift.

International Heritage Centre and Museum

BASED at William Booth College, Denmark Hill, the International Heritage Centre tells the story of The Salvation Army from its origins in the 1860s to the present day, both in the UK and overseas.

The Heritage Centre includes a library, archive and museum where specialist archivists collect, preserve, catalogue, research and make accessible material about the life and work of the Army.

Reading Room

You'll often find people in the Reading Room, including academic researchers and Salvation Army cadets training for ministry at William Booth College.

Museum

The Salvation Army museum explores the origins of the Movement and the lives of the early Salvationists, including the persecution they suffered. It also charts such things as the Army's musical heritage, the role played during conflict, its global expansion and its commitment to social justice. Entry is free for everyone.

In October 2011 an open evening was held at the new museum specifically for archivists and curators keen to see the new facilities.

Those interested in the history of The Salvation Army can also visit The William Booth Birthplace Museum in Notintone Place, Sneinton in Nottingham. The Birthplace Museum is the house where William Booth was born in 1829.

Hadleigh Farm and Training Centre

I N 1890 William Booth established a farm colony on land in Hadleigh in Essex where unskilled and less fortunate people, mostly from the East End of London, received practical training to prepare them for work and a better life. 'Work for All' was a key theme of General Booth's book *In Darkest England and the Way Out*.

Today, Hadleigh still operates as a small working farm, which includes a Rare Breeds Centre, but the predominant work on the site is the training centre where around 150 students, many with learning difficulties, receive specialist education.

In August 2012 Hadleigh Farm will host the Olympic Mountain Bike event – the course will be a lasting legacy for the community.

At Hadleigh Training Centre there's education in everything from horticulture, animal husbandry, estates management and carpentry, to information technology and graphics, catering and retail. The public tearoom gives students practical experience in hospitality and, with the Rare Breeds Centre, attracts thousands of visitors to Hadleigh every year.

'Training people for life'

William Booth

Leicester South
hall complex

Leicester South

T HE Army's Leicester South Corps is a busy place.

Based in a suite of buildings in the South Wigston part of the city, it's one of several Army centres across Leicester. The corps is typical in that it's not just about Sunday worship but also daily mission and activities for the community where everyone is welcome. Here are a few highlights from a month at Leicester South.

Paul Boyer and Bob Markham maintain the grounds around the corps building.

Giles Coulters, who's also a bandsman at the corps, is the official cleaner.

Friendly welcome

The Leicester South Corps restaurant is open Monday to Friday offering light meals at excellent prices.

Salvo Band

In addition to the main brass band at the corps, Leicester South also hosts Salvo Band, which was formed around ten years ago to play in the villages around Birmingham. It consists mainly of Salvationists and Christian friends who rehearse weekly and give three charity concerts a year.

Forward Looking Club

The corps welcomes people of all ages and among the regular activities are the weekly Forward Looking Club for over 55s and carpet bowls.

Scrabble Club

One of the more unusual activities is the Scrabble Club, which started around five years ago in a private home. As the club has grown it has moved into the corps building, with around 20 people attending every week.

Little Conquerors

There's also a fantastic parent-and-toddler group called Little Conquerors (above). Every Thursday up to 70 children and more than 50 parents attend and everyone has enormous fun.

Worship

Of course there's Sunday worship at Leicester South. There's a warm welcome at the door before the meeting and the band and songsters are among those who contribute to the all-age worship. And there's always a time of fellowship over tea and coffee after worship.

More than a place to stay

SALVATION Army Lifehouses, which provide accommodation-based supported housing, are much more than just a bed for the night. Most service users spend up to two years at a Lifehouse, receiving assistance from professional staff for issues such as physical and mental health challenges or a breakdown in relationships.

Devonport House, in the docks area of Plymouth, provides accommodation and support to 72 homeless men. There are opportunities for education and a range of other activities, with volunteers from the community playing a important part in the life of the centre. All service users are encouraged to maximise their potential, become self-confident and eventually live independently.

Catering

Homeless people often suffer from poor nutrition. Lyndsey (previous page, far left) is a volunteer teacher at Devonport House, running cooking and nutrition classes. For some residents, preparing and eating food together is an enjoyable activity, while for others it has been the first step in improving their health and independence.

With support from the NHS, Lyndsey doubled the frequency of her classes to twice-weekly and is also offering a healthy eating session for 18- to 25-year-olds – a particularly vulnerable group. In the first six months service users reported greater confidence and improved communication and team-building skills.

Some have secured work or apprenticeships in the food industry, two are training with the Prince's Trust and several more are hoping to study catering at local colleges.

The Boat Project

Devonport House has a 28-foot Bermudian sloop, donated by a former service user. Many Devonport locals are skilled boatbuilders; two shipwrights and many other service users with significant expertise came forward to work on the project.

By October 2011 the boat was completely stripped back and is now being restored to its former glory by the Lifehouse service users, with materials donated by local companies and individuals.

'Restoration is stage one of the project. Already our local MP has expressed an interest in being involved in the launch and taking a trip around Plymouth.'
Major Lynden Gibbs, Centre Manager Devonport House Lifehouse

Donations welcomed

A Devonport House service user sorts and stores tins and dried food donated by local churches, schools and other interest groups. The food is a lifeline as it is handed out in food parcels to people moving out of the centre into independent living.

The workshop

Max is a modern-day hero who has volunteered at Devonport House workshop twice a week for the past 12 years. He's a member of the local Wood Turner's Guild and in retirement decided he wanted to pass his skills onto service users at the centre.

Staff training

Staff as well as service users need opportunities to develop. Here a long-term member of Devonport House staff is introduced to the complexities of modern technology as the catering team learn the basics of computer ordering.

From the Isle of Man...

THE Salvation Army United Kingdom Territory with the Republic of Ireland includes offshore corps and communities including the Channel Islands – Jersey, Guernsey and Alderney – and the Isle of Man.

Noah's Ark Nursery is a small community nursery in Laxley on the Isle of Man and is part of Douglas Corps. Here the children enjoy learning, whether it be listening to stories or playing. Every day staff try to take the children out – a trip to the park or the beach – to help them learn more about their surroundings and notice changes in their environment. Waving to yachts leaving the harbour is a favourite activity.

IN November 1874 the work began in Wales and today The Salvation Army has corps and social programmes in both North and South Wales.

Although numerically small, the corps in Llantwit Fardre in South Wales makes a great impact on the community, particularly with young people and children.

Llantwit Fardre's Soul Fusion group is for children and youth from churches across the area and in Autumn 2011 they ran a series of events called Superhero based on the popular Angry Birds game. This proved a hit with young people who would not normally go to church.

...to South Wales

From Ireland...

 HE Salvation Army opened in Ireland in 1880 and today has churches and social centres across Northern Ireland and in the Republic.

York House Lifehouse in Dublin is one of four residential centres in the city where 80 residents are supported. The Daily Living Skills course is an interactive 12-week programme where clients master basic living skills ranging from cooking, washing and budgeting to dealing with tenancies or loneliness.

Major Marjory Parrott is Programme Co-ordinator at York House

...to Scotland

 HE first corps opened in Scotland in March 1879 and Salvation Army outreach, mission and worship is still strong, whether it be teaching and singing with the 'wee ones' in a parent-and-toddler group in Arbroath or enjoying all-age Sunday worship at Glenrothes Corps in Fife.

77

THE Salvation Army has an extensive network of chaplains across the UK and Republic of Ireland. They serve in nearly 30 fields including prisons, ports, waterways, hospitals and universities. At airports such as Heathrow and Gatwick they are usually part of larger faith chaplaincy groups.

In the Republic of Ireland Major John Parrott has been chaplain to the Dublin Ports since October 2007, providing pastoral and spiritual support to staff and passengers at Dublin airport and Dublin ferry ports and commercial docklands.

'Airports are by nature confusing, noisy and sometimes scary places,' says John. 'Serving the public and port authority staff is my spiritual ministry; I see it being the "presence of Christ" when people are experiencing difficulties, joys, sadness, relief and loneliness. When they need a prayer, a shoulder for reassurance, a comforting word, or just a smile to help them on their way, I'm there.

'Isn't this what Jesus would do?' he asks. 'Recently someone said, "Chaplain John is our church on the frontline." It's not just a job for me, my badge says what I'm about. The Salvation Army does this "Because Someone Cares".'

Public

'Your days at the most cannot be very long, so use them to the best of your ability for the glory of God and the benefit of your generation'

William Booth

RIGHT
Major John Parrott is Community Chaplain to Dublin International Airport and Port.

Public affairs
The Salvation Army at Parliament

 ILLIAM and Catherine Booth, founders of The Salvation Army, believed fighting for social justice was an essential part of Christianity. Early Salvationists, as champions of the most marginalised and vulnerable members of society, were committed not just to helping people but to advocating on their behalf at the highest levels.

Today, building on that legacy and a century of social justice work, the Public Affairs Unit builds relationships at every level of government, including local councils and Westminster. Working directly with government committees and liaising with other organisations, the Army is able to give input regarding important social policy issues facing the UK in the 21st century.

All Party Parliamentary Group on Poverty

The Army provides secretariat services to the UK All Party Parliamentary Group on Poverty. This group met for its inaugural lecture in the House of Commons during October 2011, coinciding with the United Nations Day for the Eradication of Poverty.

Representatives from a Salvation Army addictions centre and other charities tackling poverty in their communities met with Iain Duncan Smith MP, Secretary of State for Work and Pensions. The inset shows Mr Smith standing, centre, with Susan Tollington, Centre Manager, Gloucester House (seated, right) and Dr Helen Cameron, the Army's Head of Public Affairs, far right.

Party conferences

The Salvation Army attends all the major annual political party conferences as part of a wider church delegation, meeting ministers and other political leaders, and decision and policy makers.

At the 2011 Conservative Party Conference in Manchester, Dr Helen Cameron, Head of Public Affairs (front right) is seen with other church leaders and (centre) Eric Pickles, Secretary of State for Communities and Local Government and MP for Brentwood and Ongar.

New Direction Braintree

Brooks Newmark, MP for Braintree, is pictured (above left) with Sharon Ralph (Project Manager, New Direction Lifehouse), Debbie Thomas (Assistant Regional Manager, London Region) and Corps Sergeant-Major David Mann (Braintree Corps).

Tŷ Gobaith

Alun Michael, MP for Cardiff South and Penarth, is pictured (centre) during a visit to Tŷ Gobaith Lifehouse in Cardiff, where he met service users and staff.

'The Salvation Army staff do amazing work. It's been a privilege to visit. Spending time here has shown me that the dedication of the staff and their work to provide training, rebuild relationships and get people into a place of their own makes a huge difference which benefits us all'

Brooks Newmark MP

Chelmsford

In October 2011 Stephen Timms, MP for East Ham and a prominent Christian politician, was the guest for a Sunday afternoon celebration at Chelmsford Corps in Essex. Mr Timms spoke about his Christian faith and how it has influenced his work as an MP and government minister. Mr Timms is seen here with corps officer Major Susan Jones.

MPs visit Lifehouses

Ben Gummer (second from right), MP for Ipswich, visited Lyndon House Lifehouse in his constituency. He met Rebecca Hunn (Duty Manager, Lyndon House), Andy Woodhouse (Assistant Regional Manager, London) and Major David Jackson, Divisional Commander, Anglia.

Vale Street Stoke-on-Trent

Dr Tristram Hunt, MP for Stoke-on-Trent Central (centre), was welcomed to Vale Street Lifehouse. He is seen here with service user Andrew Carter, Centre Manager Gary Thomas, service user Rory Clarke and Major Samuel Edgar, Divisional Commander, West Midlands.

Media moments
Spotlight on the Army

SALVATION Army work and people are often featured in the media at local, regional and national levels. At Christmas it's not uncommon to see the Army in a TV drama and, when musicians are involved, producers often like to use actual Salvationists to ensure authenticity of sound and appearance.

These shows are filmed well in advance, so in October 2011 a group of bandsmen and women visited the set of the BBC's *EastEnders* to record part of an episode for Christmas 2011. During breaks in filming they enjoyed meeting cast members and visiting landmarks familiar to viewers of the long-running drama.

Open-air ministry
Taking the good news to the streets

WILLIAM and Catherine Booth believed in taking the Christian gospel to the people – not expecting everyone to come to church.

In 1865 the East London Christian Mission – later to be renamed The Salvation Army – began with an open-air tent meeting on Mile End Waste in East London.

Despite early opposition, the Army has been taking to the streets ever since.

Regent Hall Band marches through central London from its worship centre in Oxford Street.

> 'You are to preach to them in such a way as will cause them to look and listen'
>
> Catherine Booth

Central London

The Salvation Army Regent Hall is the only church on Oxford Street. Every Sunday the Christian message is proclaimed with an open-air meeting and a march of witness.

Birmingham

Birmingham Citadel witnesses to thousands of people every year in the city centre.

Across the country

Salvation Army outdoor services take place every week, and sometimes include a march of witness through the streets.

1. Colchester Citadel
2. Winton, Bournemouth
3. Felixstowe
4. Willingham
5. Coventry

Colchester

Open-air ministry is a great opportunity that sometimes leads to people becoming more interested in attending church services. In October 2011 Norwich Mile Cross Band visited Colchester Citadel and the two corps joined forces to take to the streets.

Publishing

Communicating the
good news of God

HE Publishing Department at the Army's Territorial Headquarters in London produces periodicals, books and other printed materials.

The War Cry and *Kids Alive!* — both full-colour, weekly newspapers — are sold on the streets and in Army centres around the UK and the Republic of Ireland. *Salvationist,* also produced weekly and in full colour, is a paper for Salvation Army members and friends.

The War Cry

It's all in the forward planning - Major Nigel Bovey, Editor of *The War Cry* and team plan future editions of the popular weekly paper (above)

Kids Alive!

Editor Justin Reeves and graphic designer Rodney Kingston deep in conversation about the next issue of Britain's only weekly Christian kids comic.

'Weekly deadlines make for busy people, so careful planning and skilled personnel are vital. However, like anyone producing newspapers, we must be ready at a moment's notice to adjust our plans according to what's happening in the world. Our aim is to communicate the good news of God at work in the world in the most up-to-date, interesting and professional way possible.'

Major Leanne Ruthven, Editor-in-Chief

Print and Design

(Above and right) The Print and Design Unit produces much of the Army's requirements for printed material: books, manuals, booklets, brochures, business cards, letterheads, posters and more.

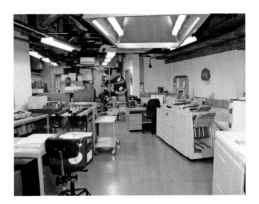

Salvationist

Major Stephen Poxon, Editor, and Major Philippa Smale, Literary Editor, discuss an important issue.

Good News
*Changing lives through
'The War Cry'*

WILLIAM Booth believed in the power of the printed word and in the value of writers whose 'pens are dipped in the love of God'. From the early days he produced newspapers aimed at informing, inspiring and challenging readers.

The first edition of the Army's flagship newspaper *The War Cry* was published in 1879 and today the paper is still being sold in high streets, markets and pubs across the country. It's a way of bringing the good news about Jesus Christ to those who might not hear it any other way.

Roy Dainty (above) first came into contact with The Salvation Army when he bought a copy of *The War Cry*. What he read challenged him to think about faith and eventually he started attending the local corps. He became a Christian and, subsequently, a *War Cry* seller.

Roy now leads the corps at Arbroath in north Scotland. He still sells *The War Cry* every week and shares his faith with all who stop to talk. A simple decision to buy a newspaper changed his life.

Upminster

Lloyds TSB Bank plc

'Pens dipped in the love of God'

William Booth

Good news in Romford

The Romford *War Cry* team in Essex includes Andy (above) and Gillian (right). Tom and Geoff meet for a strategic chat (below) before hitting the streets and meeting customers (left).

Emergency Services

Crisis and disaster response and support

THE Salvation Army seeks to alleviate distress wherever it is found and often, when there is a fire, railway or airport incident or civil emergency, you'll find the Army's mobile canteen units. These purpose-built vehicles are staffed largely by Salvation Army volunteers from the local area who provide practical and emotional support to emergency services personnel.

The Army also offers places of safety for people who are evacuated from their homes and personnel to provide both immediate and ongoing support. Specially-trained emergency services teams may also be involved at designated rest centres, humanitarian assistance centres or mortuary viewing areas, where they provide faith support as appropriate.

In October 2011 personnel from Central North Division supported around 100 people during Exercise Aliquot (above), a mass decontamination exercise. This involved fire and rescue units from Cheshire and Manchester, Cheshire Police and the North West Ambulance Service Hazardous Area Response Team.

Stowmarket

Stowmarket team in Suffolk supported emergency services staff responding to a large thatched farmhouse fire (above).

Manchester

Central North Division team offered assistance at a large fire in a Manchester furnishing store (right). They served around 70 fire personnel, police, ambulance and utility workers, including firefighters John Crawley (left) and Steve Thomas.

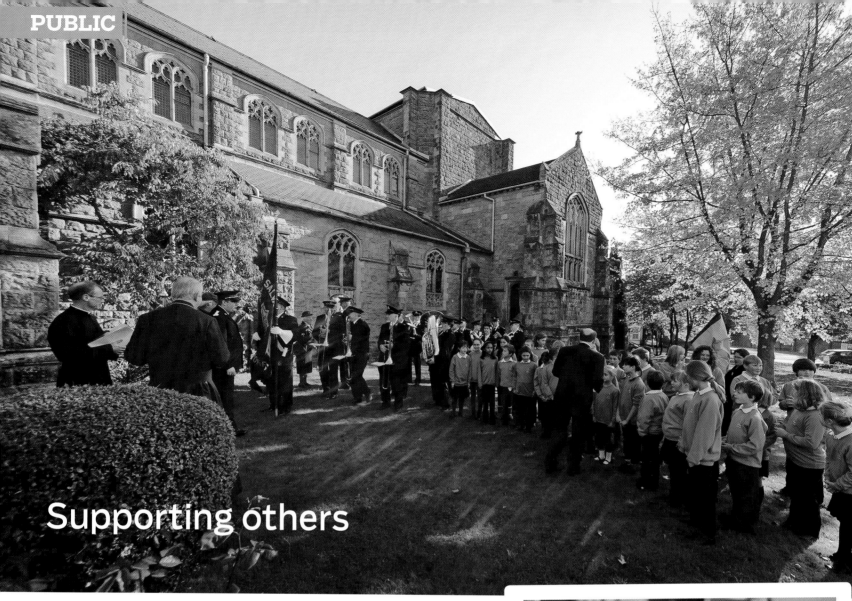

Supporting others

THE Army is privileged to support community and civic occasions and its musicians are regularly called upon to take part in public ceremonies and fundraising events.

On Remembrance Sunday you will usually find an Army band providing music at the Cenotaph, and during October 2011 the Army had many opportunities to support other organisations.

Welcoming a new bishop

Members of Salisbury Band and personnel from the Army's Southern Division marched the new Church of England Bishop of Salisbury, the Right Reverend Nicholas Holtam, through the streets of the city before his enthronement. The bishop said prayers for the city en route and hymns were sung as the procession made its way to the cathedral.

Fundraising in Blackpool

Blackpool Citadel has a long relationship with St Christopher's Church in the south of the town. For the last two years the band and songsters have visited the church to present a fundraising event. Pictured is an energetic timbrel display.

Memorial for a heroine

Edith Cavell was a First World War heroine from Norfolk and every year a service is held in her honour at Norwich Cathedral. The Army band from Norwich Mile Cross Corps, one of two Salvation Army centres in the city, has supported this event for several years. This event was particularly poignant in 2011 as it took place during the 90th Anniversary Year of the British Legion who are also always out in force on the day.

October saw a first for Bedlington Band (below), playing Christmas carols while supporting a wonderful cause – the National Society for the Prevention of Cruelty to Children.

Celebrities in Chichester

Worthing Band presented Music for an Autumn Evening in Chichester Cathedral, with TV actress Patricia Routledge (left).

Leprosy Mission concert

Coventry City Band presented a Festival of Music in aid of the Leprosy Mission at St Nicholas Church, Kenilworth, in Warwickshire, raising over £900 (above).

Climbing Everest for others

In 2011 a team of intrepid Salvation Army fundraisers trekked the Himalayas, enduring two weeks of gruelling hiking and climbing, high winds and high altitude. Reaching Everest Base Camp on 13 October, they raised more than £36,000 for various Salvation Army projects.

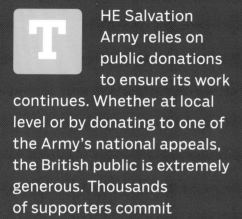

THE Salvation Army relies on public donations to ensure its work continues. Whether at local level or by donating to one of the Army's national appeals, the British public is extremely generous. Thousands of supporters commit themselves to giving regular financial donations and it is always a privilege when someone remembers The Salvation Army in their will.

National fundraising is managed by a small, dedicated team based at Territorial Headquarters in London. They are also available to advise those arranging local fundraising efforts across the country.

The Trusts Unit works with funding trusts to support individual Salvation Army projects throughout the UK and the Republic of Ireland. It also encourages people to raise money through various events, which was how the Everest Base Camp Challenge came about. Hengi Bayat, Funding Development Manager in the Trusts Unit, and a small group of trekkers spent two weeks in October 2011 climbing to base camp, an altitude of 5,364 metres.

'I wanted to complete a challenge which was out of the ordinary and would stay with me for a long time. I will be able to talk to my three sons about it and inspire them to do more. I also wanted to raise funds for our community work in Fitton Hill in Oldham, a place that has huge potential for the future.'

Chris Neilson, Everest Challenge team member

'The funds I'm raising are going towards Older People's Services, which provide loving, secure environments for older people in what can sometimes be tight financial circumstances. I've been inspired by the caring nature of the staff and their willingness to serve the residents. Not everyone can afford such care, and The Salvation Army tops up local authority funding to ensure a consistent level of care is received by all.'
Fleur Bragaglia, researcher in the Army's national Research and Development Department.

Grassroots support
Raising funds at local level

IN addition to national fundraising, the proceeds of which are distributed to projects and communities across the United Kingdom and Republic of Ireland, Salvation Army corps also fundraise locally, particularly during the Annual Appeal in September.

Christmas starts early for the Army, with October heralding the launch of the Christmas Present Appeal, when celebrities, dignitaries, businesses, schools and churches provide thousands of toys for distribution across the country.

In at least one centre – Knottingley – October 2011 saw the band playing carols at a local garden centre (middle right).

Fundraising together
In Yorkshire, Knottingley Salvation Army has a band but no town centre where they can collect funds. Nearby Pontefract Corps has a town centre but no band, so the two help each other out. Here they are (above) in The Buttercross, Pontefract Market Place, for a special collection day.

Christmas Present Appeal
In Chesterton, Staffordshire, Christmas Appeal Co-ordinator Teresa Dunn was voted a Local Hero for her work. A large cut-out of her was displayed at the Britannia Building Society/ Stoke Sentinel Awards Night. Teresa is pictured in October (right) with her cut-out at the launch of the appeal.

At Peterborough Citadel members of the day centre prepare Christmas boxes full of gifts during October.

Salvation Army Trading Company

HE Army's public face also includes charity shops, recycling banks and other outlets where funds are raised for local projects.

Salvation Army Trading Company Ltd (SATCoL), a subsidiary of the Army, operates a nationwide network of shops and a national textile recycling scheme. Millions of pounds of profit are given back to the Army annually to support its work.

Charity shops

Army charity shops employ staff and volunteers who, as well as assisting with sales, offer help and advice where needed. In October 2011 a new shop opened in Stranraer in West Scotland (above).

SP&S

Salvationist Publishing & Supplies (SP&S), which sells such things as uniforms, books and music, is part of SATCoL's operations. In October the shop held a sale day and coffee morning which raised more than £150 for Macmillan Cancer Support. There was entertainment from a small group of Army musicians, and the event even drew some international visitors, including a small contingent on holiday from Norway (top right).

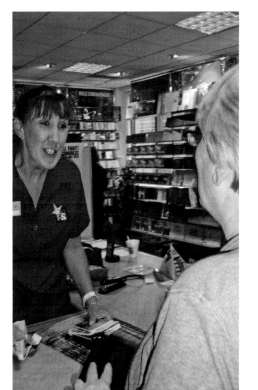

Recycling

More than 30,000 tonnes of clothing, shoes and other items are placed in Salvation Army recycling banks every year. SATCoL works with local authorities and key businesses to ensure good recycling practices.

Sharing the message
Through media

GENERAL William Booth believed that to spread the Christian message, The Salvation Army needed to make use of the latest technology. He encouraged early Salvationists to have their photographs taken and regularly spoke to journalists to ensure the Army featured in the newspapers. In 2012 The Salvation Army is still making headlines and has embraced social media including Facebook, Twitter and YouTube. The Army's Video Production Unit helps tell the story of what's happening in the UK and internationally.

In October 2011 the unit visited Haiti to see the progress made since the January 2010 earthquake which devastated this already impoverished nation. The Army has been established as a church and charity in Haiti since 1950 and, despite losing many of its own buildings in the earthquake, quickly responded to the community's needs through its network of corps, schools and health clinics.

High shot

It's all in the line of duty for The Salvation Army. During filming cameraman Neil McInnes (below) found some interesting places from which to shoot.

Hope for the future

Sebastian (pictured back right and below) attends a Salvation Army school in Port-au-Prince. He lives with his family in a small tent in the Place de la Paix, a camp on the football pitch behind the school. Despite the poverty in which he lives, 13-year-old Sebastian dreams of the future – he wants to be a pilot or a doctor.

Rebuilding

At College Varena in Port-au-Prince pupils study in a temporary classroom (above). The site, which included the Army's regional headquarters and corps, was extensively damaged in the 2010 earthquake. Rebuilding is now under way here and at Laferronnay School on the outskirts of the city (right).

Food supplies

The Army distributes food to its 48 schools in Haiti; for many of the children it's their only meal of the day. Road conditions aren't good but the support for the schools, clinics and churches is vital to everyday survival.

THE Salvation Army's practical hands-on work is renowned. It has never been enough just to preach; the message of God's love is also demonstrated through its work, particularly with marginalised and vulnerable people.

The Army's ministry to the older generation extends across the nation with a network of 16 residential care homes and a number of day centres, as well as corps-based activities, luncheon clubs and support groups. The aim is to treat older people with dignity, to recognise the value they bring to community life and to help make later life a time of fulfilment. We aim to assist them to remain independent for as long as possible and, when needed, to provide high-quality care.

Practical

'Faith and works should travel side by side, step answering to step, like the legs of men walking. First faith, and then works; and then faith again, and then works again, until you can scarcely distinguish which is the one and which is the other.'

William Booth

RIGHT
Sandra Sneddon is manager at the Army's Eva Burrows Day Centre in Cambuslang, Scotland. Here a seven-strong team cares for around 50 regular visitors aged between 67 and 94, most of whom have been diagnosed with some form of dementia.

Caring for older people

THE Eva Burrows Day Centre opened in 2000 and has become an important part of life for many older people living in the Cambuslang area. The centre is open each weekday and offers support, companionship and activities.

There's always food, someone to chat to and even a little light exercise – all in the care of dedicated staff. There are also activities where partners are invited, including games, guest speakers, tea dances and day trips.

The service also provides family members and carers with respite – they can go shopping, take part in other activities, or just have time to themselves.

Sometimes people living in care homes visit the day centre for lunch and, on return visits, day centre clients are given an insight into life in a care home.

'The Eva Burrows Day Centre is a wonderful place to be. I am passionate about my work. We work on a Christian basis and have a chaplain because spirituality is important to most of our clients. We try to make everyone feel special and treat all with the respect and dignity they deserve.

   'Most of all we try to be there for anyone who wants to talk, sit quietly or maybe share a prayer. When someone turns to you and tells you they had a good day, it makes my job worthwhile. I want all who use the service to be happy, content and know they are welcome.'

Sandra Sneddon

Memories

The Reminiscence Room at the Eva Burrows Day Centre is filled with familiar items from the past. People living with dementia often remember things from their distant past and talking about these items assists this process.

   Looking at old pictures of Cambuslang and Glasgow always starts conversations about the days when people lived in the 'toon', or when they used boards in the wash house, laughing while scrubbing the 'bairns' clothes'.

Sharing a quiet mom[e]
at Smallcombe Hou
Ba[

Dignity and respect

HE Army provides high-quality residential care for several hundred older people from diverse cultures who can no longer live independently in their own homes. They are looked after by trained carers who treat them with the dignity and respect they deserve.

The approach is holistic, caring for physical, intellectual, social, cultural and spiritual needs. Each home has a chaplain who offers support to staff, residents and their families.

'When I have the privilege of visiting one of our older people's homes I always ask myself, "Would my mother be happy here? Would she feel safe?" Surroundings can be made clean and comfortable and the Army works hard to create stable, stimulating environments to meet essential standards. But it's people who make a home happy. It's people who make a home feel safe.'

Dean Juster, Territorial Safeguarding Officer

Bradbury Care Home

'Our Reminiscence Room is used on a daily basis and is full of objects that promote conversation and memory recall. Staff members add objects to this room all the time – it is like a living museum – and the residents like to see and handle the items from the past.'

Lawrence Taylor, Manager, Bradbury Care Home, Southend-on-Sea

In 2010 Bradbury Care Home received a small legacy from a former resident. The woman wanted to create a Reminiscence Room for the benefit of all the residents, so an unused bathroom was converted into this special space. Here Edith Sinclair and chaplain Envoy Janet Annan are pictured talking about old photos.

Smallcombe House, Bath

At Smallcombe House Care Home in Bath, as with all Army residential care homes, there's a happy, compassionate, nurturing atmosphere. Care Home Manager Ena Caddy, seen at her desk (top), heads up a hard-working, happy team, one of whom is pictured above.

Helping others

BEING homeless can be devastating and is often associated with other problems such as addictions and mental health challenges. Those who access Salvation Army programmes are encouraged to help others in practical ways, some of which are demonstrated here.

HOPE volunteers

The HOPE project – Helping Other Projects Evolve – began at Witham Lodge Lifehouse in Skegness and is now operating at many of the Army's centres. Volunteers undertake supervised work in their communities and in October 2011 some laid concrete at a sanctuary for greyhounds (top and bottom left), while others did some essential gardening for members of the community (top right). They also helped on a soup run for people living rough (bottom right). Many Salvation Army service users have experienced this life and know what a hot drink on a cold night means.

Swan Lodge
Sunderland

HOPE Volunteers from Swan Lodge took part in gardening projects during October 2011, when they trimmed a hedgerow and cleared garden borders for elderly members of their community.

Eva Burrows
1st Stop Project

This project in Cambuslang, Scotland, accommodates people who are waiting to move into new tenancies. Here staff and service users paint and decorate a flat ready for use.

Chickens and scooters at Salisbury House

CTOBER 2011 saw the arrival of two new 'residents' at Salisbury House Lifehouse in St Helens – chickens named Sali and Jemima. Service users and staff built the coop and now look after their new charges. The first egg was laid in November and they are now planning to build a bigger structure to keep up to six chickens.

Salisbury House centre manager Robert Long (above right) encourages activities that are fun but which also provide practical skills. He donated a scooter, one of two that service users stripped and rebuilt. Having passed roadworthiness tests, the scooters will be sold in order to buy others needing restoration.

Other practical activities at the centre include the building of a polytunnel, where herbs and vegetables are now grown.

Hands on

 N many Army corps and centres people enjoy practical activities such as craft and art. There are regular clubs for people of all ages where creativity is encouraged.

Not only is this great fun but in some instances items produced also help others in the local community and further afield.

Expert knitters

Cameo Club members in Romford enjoy knitting time (above), while Home League members in Luton (above right) knit shawls and pray for those who will receive them: babies in the local neonatal unit, families with newborns or people suffering ill health.

At Upper Norwood expert knitter Jenny (right) is hard at work, as are those at Leicester South Arts and Craft Club (left).

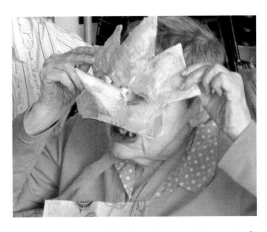

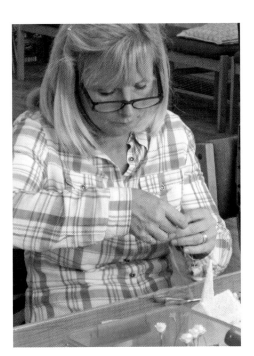

World of Art and SugarCraft classes in Taunton, Somerset.

Arts and crafts at Blackpool Citadel.

Support for communities

P EOPLE often turn to The Salvation Army when they find it hard to make ends meet. In the recent difficult economic circumstances, the help provided by local corps has become a lifeline for many people.

Thousands of food parcels are distributed every year and many Army centres work with other food distribution charities to ensure people in immediate need are helped. The Army is also privileged to receive food donations from the pubic as well as many supermarkets and other food outlets.

Blackpool

Blackpool Citadel's Bridge Project supports vulnerable and homeless people. In October 2011 Corps Community Manager Roy Powers received donations from Lytham Hall Park Primary School's head teacher Mrs Carolyn Vickers (right).

Harvest treats are donated for Winton's meal run for homeless people.

Food Bank

Worthing Salvation Army and the Jubilee Community Church help people going through short-term crises. The Food Bank operates every weekday afternoon and is staffed by volunteers, seen here on a break.

Kind kids

At Grazebrook Primary School in Stoke Newington, Hackney, children made a special harvest food donation to the Army.

'The growing demand for food parcels is an increasing issue in our community and we see the Mustard Tree Allotment as nature's way of being able to help meet that need. We are grateful to other churches – St Margaret's and Aspley Evangelical Church – who helped us top up our food store over the summer.'

Lieutenant Matt Elsey (left), Corps Officer, Nottingham Aspley

Mustard Tree Allotment

Nottingham Aspley Corps not only helps people in the community with food, they grow it.

Ian Piper and Sandra Ferguson, friends of the corps, planned and planted much of the allotment, which produces organic fruit and vegetables to help meet a growing demand for food parcels for those struggling to make ends meet.

In October 2011 the Mustard Tree Allotment was the site of a thanksgiving service as Salvation Army members and friends gave thanks for the year's harvest.

Produce is also used in the corps café, while some is sold at Aspley's Miles Better local market. Many volunteers, including children, are involved in the project.

Anyone for lunch?

Lunch with a friend at Southsea Citadel's Lighthouse Community Café, open six days a week.

Food glorious food

E VERY week, in Salvation Army centres across the UK and Republic of Ireland, thousands of people enjoy lunch and other home-cooked meals. Many places run not-for-profit drop-in cafés and there are luncheon clubs and other services providing nutritious, low-cost meals. For many who attend this may be their one substantial meal for the week. In many corps, lunch follows or precedes an activity – many members of Cameo clubs start with lunch. It's an opportunity not just to enjoy good food, but also to meet friends.

Norwich Mile Cross

The Luncheon Club at Norwich Mile Cross began 28 years ago and for many years was run solely by volunteers who cooked the meals and served, transported, visited and supported needy folk in the area. When the day centre opened around ten years ago the corps employed a full-time cook but the service still relies on volunteers. Corps officer Major David Murray (above) is also on hand to share a word.

Bedlington

Here a popular lunch club meets every week.

Colchester Citadel

Major David House (centre) and members of the Luncheon Club kitchen team prepare a nutritious meal. Wednesday lunch originally commenced to provide a link between the morning Bowls Club and the afternoon Friendship Club.

Aberdeen Citadel

The corps café is open five days a week, offering food to happy visitors.

Romford

In October 2011 staff at Romford's Friendship Café held a fundraising event for Breast Cancer Awareness.

Liverpool Bootle

The drop-in centre and charity shop is open three days a week providing free breakfast for homeless people and low-cost lunches for the general public. There are shower and laundry facilities available for homeless people and those on low incomes.

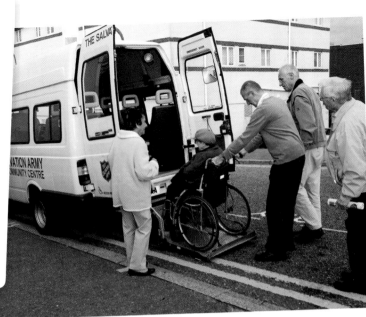

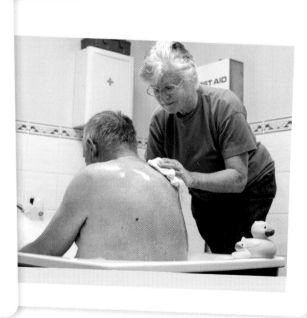

The Place Next Door
Practical Christian love

THE Salvation Army at Winton in Bournemouth runs a community programme that includes a luncheon club, hairdressing services and chiropody clinic. Twenty years ago the corps put its faith into action and, working with other organisations in Bournemouth, raised funds to buy an old ice cream factory next door to the Salvation Army hall.

Today The Place Next Door is a busy centre with full-time staff and hundreds of volunteers. The building is also used by other organisations and is the base for a street feeding programme and other vital services for families and marginalised people. And it's also a safe, fun place for young people from the community.

An international Army
Practical support across the world

THE Salvation Army operates in thousands of impoverished communities around the world. In many places the Army is a growing church with a strong Christian presence. It could be said that, internationally, the Army doesn't just help the poor, it is predominantly made up of people who *are* poor.

Thanks to those who help raise hundreds of thousands of pounds a year, Salvation Army International Development (SAID) in the UK directly supports many overseas communities, providing clean water, health, agriculture and education programmes. The emphasis is always on supporting and empowering people to build better lives for themselves. SAID UK also raises awareness of social justice issues including anti-human trafficking and fair trade.

'Life with dignity, equality for all people and a world without poverty and injustice'

The Salvation Army International Development UK vision statement

SAMIDE Project

SAMIDE - The Salvation Army Micro-Credit Development project in Tanzania, East Africa – enables people to receive small business loans. These allow them to increase their household incomes and meet such things as school and medical costs for their children. In October 2011 SAID UK project officers visited the Tabora and Mbeya areas to see how the businesses were progressing. Pictured is a co-worker from Australia.

Protecting the vulnerable

The Army partners with anti-human trafficking group Stop The Traffik in its Freedom Ticket for Life campaign, which works to protect vulnerable girls and women. In Mbagala, on the outskirts of Dar-es-Salaam, Tanzania, there are two homes for 40 girls between the ages of 7 and 18. Here they receive an education which keeps them off the streets, decreasing their likelihood of being trafficked.

There's also practical support including group counselling and life skills training – everything from cooking, washing and healthy living to growing food and caring for the environment. Vocational training enables these young women to find work, putting them on a path to a much brighter future.

Responding to global crises

The Army regularly responds to crises around the world. The Emergency Services Department at International Headquarters in London deploys people with expertise as needed. One of those is Major Alison Thompson, who is usually found on the staff at Central North Divisional Headquarters in Manchester.

In October 2011 Alison was part of a team that responded to the drought in northeast Uganda, where she helped deliver food to more than 1,400 households. The team was also involved in drilling boreholes in order to provide a safe, clean water source for these communities.

Left: Alison helps people with much needed food supplies.

Right: Alison with team members and villagers at a capped borehole just prior to its completion, at Korite, Uganda.

THE Salvation Army works in partnership at many levels – with local authorities, other agencies, service users and clients – to ensure the best outcomes for those it seeks to support.

The Cardiff Bus Project is an excellent example of how partnerships work. Operating out of the Army's Crichton House, this project has served rough sleepers and vulnerable people in the Welsh capital since 2002. It's an innovative way of ensuring that people have fair access to health, housing and support services.

Operating five nights a week, 52 weeks a year, it works with approximately thirty people a night, referring around seven of those to emergency accommodation. The project relies on support from the local authorities, NHS and other charitable agencies.

Partnerships

'So let us join hand-in-hand, night and day, and fight for God and souls'

William Booth

RIGHT
Catrin Howells is Project Manager of Crichton House Outreach Services.

Working together

At the heart of homelessness work in Cardiff

THE Cardiff Bus Project services include a nurse, social worker, needle exchange, advocacy and chaplaincy. Refreshments, clothes and blankets are available and the bus is equipped with medical facilities, office space, kitchen area, tumble dryers and televisions – all designed to create a homely feel and safe haven for those who use the service.

Clients may be referred to the Emergency Bed Co-ordinator, who will assess their needs and find accommodation. This may be to one of the Army's two Lifehouses in the city: Tŷ Gobaith, a 66-bed centre that caters for single people over the age of 18, or Northlands, a 24-bed facility for those aged 16 to 25. Crichton House, which operates the Bus Project, also provides 55 clients with tenancy support services, assisting them to maintain their independence.

So whatever the need and whatever the stage of homelessness a person might find themselves in, The Salvation Army in Cardiff is there for them.

'The Bus Project and the Army's social care work in Cardiff is the true essence of William Booth's mission: reaching out to those in need and engaging with them to improve their quality of life. Be it finding housing for rough sleepers, reuniting young people with their families, helping people gain qualifications while addressing substance misuse issues, or working with social services and child protection to keep families together, we are there. We fight. Every day, every night, we fight!'

Catrin Howells, Project Manager

Lifeline

The Cardiff Bus Project takes mainstream services to the streets for people with high needs. Whether it is emergency healthcare, welfare assistance or just a warm meal, the bus is a lifeline to hundreds of people in the city.

Community partnerships
Blackpool's Bridge Project

AT Blackpool Citadel the Army's Bridge Project has supported hundreds of people over the years. Many corps across the UK and Republic of Ireland provide community-based help for homeless people and those struggling with substance abuse. Many of these activities are run in partnership with council and government agencies. Everyone works together for the good of the community.

Bridging the gap

The drop-in centre at Blackpool Citadel is open four days a week, offering food, advice and referrals to other agencies. There's an NHS clinic and adult literacy classes, and the centre is also a hub where other not-for-profit organisations meet with clients.

Vulnerable people are often excluded from day-to-day activities so there are opportunities to take part in things others take for granted, such as barbecues and outings. Once a week there are sessions for chess, draughts, Scrabble, cooking and even line dancing.

Red Shield Defence Services
In partnership with the Armed Forces

F OR more than a century The Salvation Army in the UK and Republic of Ireland has worked closely with the Armed Forces, offering support to personnel on the front line, on military bases and in training camps. Red Shield Defence Services (RSDS) teams work across the UK and Germany, providing a range of services that include practical and pastoral support for families of personnel.

On some training bases the Army provides alcohol-free leisure activities and in some places also runs parent-and-toddler groups, crèches and after-school clubs.

RSDS Bovington

Bovington and Lulworth Garrison in Dorset is the home of The Royal Armoured Corps and a major training base for armoured tank personnel. Having passed out from their Phase One basic training, Phase Two trainees progress to learning more specific skills and trades, including specialist training on tanks and other fighting vehicles.

The Bovington RSDS centre is a busy community café based just outside the main barracks. It is open to the general public as well as to all sectors of the garrison. The Salvation Army also operates three mobile canteens which go into the camps and on to the driving training areas and firing ranges, serving food and drinks.

Families Day gives relatives of Phase Two trainees the opportunity to learn about various aspects of the soldiers' training.

Right: On Intake Sunday, Phase Two trainees are greeted in the Garrison Church by The Salvation Army's RSDS Bovington manager Alan Smith, who explains the support provided.

Below: Driving and Maintenance Wing trainees on their mid-morning break enjoy a welcome cuppa from Amy, one of the The Salvation Army's canteen operatives. The Driving and Maintenance Wing is one of four training schools on the base – the others being The Signals School, The Gunnery School (Lulworth) with its extended firing ranges and the Crew Training School.

'Being a Christian movement, we work closely with the chaplain (padre) and Garrison Church, supporting each other in promoting the gospel of Christ'

Alan Smith, RSDS Centre Manager, Bovington

Music Rocks
Exciting partnerships

A T Pentre Corps in South Wales an innovative partnership with the Arts Council of Wales and European social funding has resulted in a popular and successful music initiative for local teenagers.

Music Rocks began in November 2010, meeting in a local community centre, and in the first year 130 young people attended, learning how to play musical instruments and to write and record their own songs. But it's not just about fun. Many of the participants have been unemployed for more than a year, so Music Rocks is also about gaining skills and confidence which will keep them in school, training and ultimately employment. Around 95 young people have already completed enough work to be put forward for an Open College Network qualification.

In October 2011 some Music Rocks success stories were celebrated at an award ceremony. Presentations were made by Welsh Assembly Member Huw Lewis, Minister of Housing, Regeneration and Heritage, and the Mayor of Rhondda Cynon Taf.

The evening included a performance by a band made up of former Music Rocks participants. There was also an opportunity to explain Music Rocks to the minister (facing page, top).

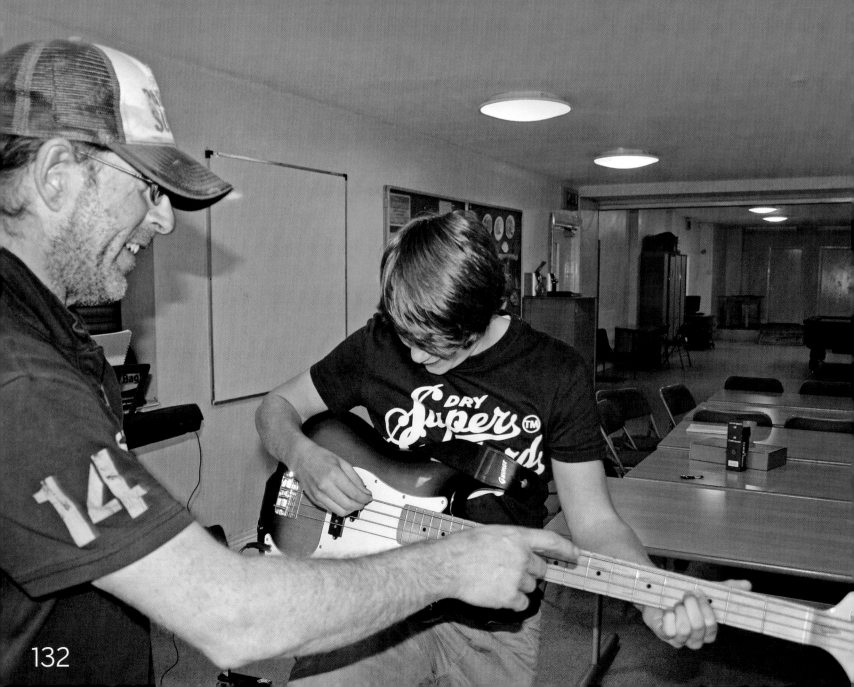

'The Salvation Army has a long and proud history of teaching children and young people to play musical instruments and Music Rocks builds on this long tradition. The instruments may be different but the benefits that come from playing with others remain.'

Mark Symonds, Strategic Development Officer for the Army's ALOVE unit, Wales.

Future funding

And the partnership continues. Further funding has been received from the Arts Council of Wales and Reach the Heights, which supports activities for young people in West Wales and the Valleys Convergence area. This secures the Music Rocks project through to January 2013.

'To be told you are never going to achieve anything in life or that you are worthless is a reality many at Swan Lodge have lived with all their lives. Well not any more! All our residents have the opportunity to succeed at the level they are capable of.'

Craig Hilton, Project Worker and Hope Volunteer Group Co-ordinator.

Lifehouse partnerships

IN many of its Lifehouses The Salvation Army works with the Salvation Army Housing Association (SAHA). This is a subsidiary of the main organisation and a national charitable Registered Provider of housing. SAHA has some general needs housing but specialises in providing supported accommodation, education and employment opportunities for homeless individuals and families.

It owns and manages many of the Army's Lifehouse buildings and works in partnership at national and local level with staff to improve the lives of service users.

Soup and a sandwich

Some service users at SAHA-owned Swan Lodge Lifehouse take part in the Soup and A Sandwich project, serving food at two corps in Sunderland. This project operates at lunchtime on Mondays and Tuesdays and the sandwiches have proved a great success, with freshly baked Lifehouse cupcakes also available.

Create

The Create Programme is a 12-week hospitality course where Swan Lodge Lifehouse service users learn cooking, customer service, food hygiene, food preparation and service skills. The course empowers confidence, team work, communication skills, creativity, commitment, discipline and fun. At the end of the course – which is backed by Morrisons supermarket – service users are more likely to find employment.

Comic book creation

Six Swan Lodge service users, along with tutor Sean Robson, wanted to create a comic book that would grab the imagination of their colleagues and eventually be shared with other agencies. The team worked on storyboards, photography and the comic strip process. The book (right) highlights issues surrounding homelessness and the prejudices service users often have to overcome.

As one service user says, 'Swan Lodge is a place of fun and laughter and that should be shown in the book'.

Hope for the future
Life at Tŷ Gobaith

THE name Tŷ Gobaith means 'Hope House' in Welsh, and hope is exactly what service users receive when they come to this centre in Cardiff. It's an inspirational place where people are given hope in their own abilities, hope to face their difficulties, hope for a world of possibilities and hope for the future.

Making music

Gwyneth Maycock is a resident at Tŷ Gobaith Lifehouse who has rekindled a passion for the trumpet. During her stay she has gained several National Open College Network (NOCN) qualifications.

Gareth Thomas (right) answered a call for music volunteer tutors and is now employed as a substance misuse worker.

The Music Room

The Music Room at Tŷ Gobaith has been running for around 18 months, offering music therapy and a chance to express creativity in a non-threatening way. There are lessons in music sequencing and guitar and bass, offered through the NOCN programme, qualifications which help service users realise their potential for the future.

Hardworking

Tŷ Gobaith's cook Jonathan Ward (left) and service user Glyn Burford (right) are part of a hardworking team which produces nutritious meals for the Lifehouse. Glyn has been awarded ten NOCN certificates and is also involved with Grub in a Tub.

Grub in a Tub

Tŷ Gobaith has always offered training and volunteer opportunities in hospitality. Many residents come with extensive experience in food service, so when they wanted to start a not-for-profit business, catering was the perfect choice. Grub in a Tub is managed and staffed entirely by service users who provide delicious home-cooked meals right to the customer's door. They also provide services to a variety of businesses and organisations in Cardiff. Ethical trading is at the core of Grub in a Tub and in 2012 Tŷ Gobaith hopes to open a community café and expand job opportunities even further.

Spirit and determination
Discovering each person's potential

Sunny personality

Stacey Evans (right) first came to Tŷ Gobaith on a 12-week work placement arranged by Gingerbread, a programme aimed at getting single mums back into work. Stacey's sunny personality had an immediate impact and she became a mentor for others on placement. Stacey so loved the work at Tŷ Gobaith that she applied for a part-time post and is now on staff.

Testing times for business

Following the success of Grub in a Tub, Tŷ Gobaith developed another social enterprise business called Testing One Two Three, which delivers a comprehensive electrical PAT testing service.

The not-for-profit business is run entirely by service users and volunteers who are trained to provide a professional service and offer feedback.

A different view

Craig Davies (above) is Skills Development Tutor – the department always encourages people to see themselves differently.

Suzanne Brannigan

Here's Craig with Suzanne Brannigan, a service user who has embraced the learning opportunities available. She has taking several NOCN certificates and regularly contributes art and poetry to the Tŷ Gobaith newsletter SHOUT. She will soon be taking over the design and layout of the newsletter, and also works in the onsite shop.

Mervyn Walters is Tŷ Gobaith's inspirational Deputy Centre Manager and is closely involved in the Testing One Two Three social enterprise scheme. Mervyn brings huge amounts of enthusiasm to everything he does in the Lifehouse, supporting service users and staff and providing health and safety and first-aid training.

'I've been privileged to work for The Salvation Army at Tŷ Gobaith for more than seven years and have enjoyed various roles and challenges. I manage an extremely passionate team who never think twice about going above and beyond the call of duty. What I find most inspiring is the spirit and determination of our residents.

'It's not an easy thing to look inside ourselves and face change. We are all our own worst enemies and no one can harm us quite like we can harm ourselves. To face what could be your biggest adversary, to reflect and see how things could be different and to start the journey one small step at a time is an awe-inspiring sight.

'Staff here at the centre are humbled by the strength of character displayed every day; it truly rouses the soul.'

Lee Ball (below), Manager Tŷ Gobaith Lifehouse

Here to help
Local friends and partners

N some places the Salvation Army hall is the biggest communal building around, so it's not surprising that its facilities are often used by other organisations. Whether it is education classes or meetings organised by statutory or other non-profit organisations, the Army is pleased to help out.

Fair trade

Fair trade is a social justice issue. Ensuring goods are ethically traded and that those who produce them receive fair wages are among the issues The Salvation Army is addressing around the world. The UK Army is registered as a fair trade organisation and there are a growing number of local initiatives which are developing the awareness of fair trade issues.

Tariro, a fair trade coffee house, started life in Morden in south London in 2003 and now has a branch in nearby Sutton, located in the Salvation Army building. It's a popular venue with customers, having the added benefit of knowing that what they eat and drink is ethically traded as well as delicious.

Right: At Southwick Community Project two of the senior staff – Julie Judson and Stuart Turnbull – are part of the Street Pastors team. University students making a documentary about the work of the Sunderland Street Pastors interviewed Julie and Stuart (right).

Partnerships with Street Pastors

Street Pastors is a joint church organisation set up in 2003 by the Ascension Trust in response to urban problems. Many Salvationists and friends are among the 9,000 trained street pastors across the country. Working with police, councils and other statutory bodies, teams of volunteers go into the streets at night. Their presence and support has resulted in a drop in crime in many towns and cities.

Above:	**Right:**
A commissioning service for new street pastors was held at The Salvation Army in Romford.	In October 2011 Captain Sue Camp-Richards (second from right) of Taunton Corps attended Taunton Carnival with the Street Pastors team.

Headway Luton

A close relationship has developed between the Army in Luton and Headway Luton Ltd, an organisation that supports people with an acquired brain injury. Weekly workshops including art classes are held at The Salvation Army where Headway staff and clients look after the garden, growing flowers and vegetables.

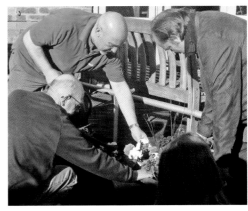

Busy Bees in Blackpool

Busy Bees is an independent pre-school nursery which uses part of the Army's complex at Blackpool Citadel. Although not directly connected to the corps, the Busy Bees have become part of the church family. Parents, children and staff are invited to services, and hold their own services to mark significant Christian events. Many of the parents also frequent Manna's Bistro – the on-site community café.

WILLIAM Booth believed that everyone had potential – they just had to be given the opportunities and training to find it. So it has never been enough for The Salvation Army just to help people with charity handouts. Wherever possible, the Army seeks to empower those with whom it works, helping them regain self-confidence and independence.

One of the ways this is achieved is through the creation of social enterprise businesses which are managed by service users themselves.

Booth House Lifehouse in Swindon provides accommodation and support for men and women who have been homeless. For several years service users at this centre have been running The Sandwich People, an award-winning catering service. Then in autumn 2011 the 'recycles' centre was launched, providing services and advice to the cycling community in Swindon.

It's projects like these that can transform the lives of the participants, giving them a hand up, not just a handout.

Possibilities

'God loves with a great love the man whose heart is bursting with a passion for the impossible'

William Booth

RIGHT
Jenna, a service user at Booth House Lifehouse in Swindon, is a member of the 'recycles' team. See her story on page 145.

A world of possibilities
Bright futures in Swindon

CUSTOMERS visiting 'recycles' bicycle centre in Swindon may not realise that the friendly, helpful staff are all residents of Booth Lifehouse next door. This is a 50-bed centre providing accommodation and support for both men and women. 'Recycles' acts as a resource centre for cycling enthusiasts in Swindon and staff are on hand to offer information about local clubs, cycling and routes, and about the benefits of the activity.

Public perceptions of homeless people can be negative, but the Army believes that 'recycles' and other social enterprise initiatives can help break those stereotypes. To be involved in social enterprise activity, Salvation Army Lifehouse service users undertake training in all aspects of the business. 'Recycles' mechanics service and repair bikes at competitive rates, and also sell quality refurbished cycles.

Jenna's story

Jenna came to Booth House in December 2010 following problems within her family. She had completed a degree in Theatre Arts, Education and Deaf studies at Reading followed by short-term contracts in care work. 'I was at a very low point in my life when I moved to Booth House, not knowing how to improve things and generally lacking confidence. Since being in Booth House, I've had the direction I needed which has helped me become a more confident person. I have volunteered in both social enterprises – The Sandwich People and 'recycles' – and gained qualifications in Food Safety, Customer Service and Sales. Currently I'm working towards a CYTECH 2 qualification in bicycle repair which is the industry-recognised qualification for cycle mechanics.' In late autumn 2011 Jenna signed a tenancy agreement to move into her own flat.

'The future is looking bright for me,' says Jenna. 'I'm very excited about moving to my own home. I know there may be difficulties ahead but I feel that I am more capable of dealing with anything I may be faced with.'

The Sandwich People

Since 2008 Booth House service users have been running The Sandwich People, an award-winning catering service.

Each weekday, made-to-order sandwiches are delivered to local businesses and, as the service has its own allotment and greenhouse, all the food offered is fresh and nutritious.

In 2010 the project won Homeless Link's Michael Whippman Award for social enterprise in the community.

Finding the missing peace
Family Tracing Service

FROM its earliest days The Salvation Army has worked with families who've drifted apart or become fractured. By 1885 the Army was already known for supporting vulnerable girls in the East End of London and families would write asking for help in tracing daughters who had left home. At first called Mrs Booth's Enquiry Agency, the work soon grew, and in 2012 the UK Family Tracing Service is one of the oldest and most successful agencies of its kind in the world.

At Territorial Headquarters a small, dedicated team of caseworkers handle more than 2,500 enquiries a year and every day the Army reunites at least eight people with long-lost family members – a success rate of almost 90%.

When families are separated, for whatever reason, it can be a source of great unhappiness. Finding one's family may not only be a way of finding the 'missing piece' but also the 'missing peace' in life. The Family Tracing Service's work in reuniting families helps bring about forgiveness, reconciliation and wholeness – all central Christian themes that are vital to the rebuilding of relationships.

THE SALVATION ARMY

FAMILY TRACING SERVICE

Finding the missing peace

Employment Plus

Helping people grow and develop

A CENTRAL theme of William Booth's vision at the turn of the 20th century was for The Salvation Army to be an organisation that helped people help themselves. He believed that providing them with opportunities to learn new skills and find work would ensure they could support themselves and their families.

In 2012 the Army's Employment Plus service works with other agencies to help people out of welfare dependency and into work, building on the Booth heritage and more than 20 years' experience delivering employment services in the UK, USA, Australia and New Zealand.

In conjunction with the UK Government, the Army works with job seekers, employers, volunteers and partner agencies, assisting people to overcome barriers to finding – and keeping – work. During October 2011 nearly 500 new starters joined Employment Plus programmes, bringing to 7,000 the total for the first 10 months of that year.

With many of its Employment Resources Centres based in Salvation Army corps buildings, the organisation is helping people help themselves.

'Work for all'

From William Booth's *In Darkest England and the Way Out* 1890

Teamwork

One Employment Plus team (left) is based in the West Midlands, and Birmingham Citadel is used as a base for interviews. To help church members better understand Employment Plus and its work, the team, including National Director Helen Robinson (centre), attended a Sunday evening service at the corps and made a presentation.

High level visit

Employment Minister Chris Grayling MP (above left) visited Bristol Bedminster Corps during October 2011 to meet customers at the Work Programme centre run by Employment Plus in partnership with Rehab Jobfit. Mr Grayling also met staff including Lynn Coutts, Employment Plus Development Manager, and Philip James, job life coach.

Staff and a job seeker meet at the Army's Employment Plus centre at Clevedon, near Bristol.

2012 and beyond
Sport and The Salvation Army

THE London Olympics and Paralympics take place in 2012 and The Salvation Army is privileged to be involved. The Army's Hadleigh Farm is the venue for the mountain bike event, where the world's best bikers will test their skills on the purpose-built track.

Corps and centres around the nation will take part in Torch Relay activities and throughout the Olympic season Salvationists will support spectators, athletes and athletes' families as part of the wider church coalition More Than Gold.

Sports ministry is a tool now being used to connect with people who might not otherwise be involved with a church, with activities for all ages groups. It's another way of spreading the good news of Jesus Christ – which is just what William Booth urged The Salvation Army to do 100 years ago.

Sport for all
Stowmarket Salvation Army Football Club (left) plays in the Suffolk and Ipswich League. Service users at Salisbury House Lifehouse in St Helens love football and have been successful at several tournaments in recent years (below) and at Colchester Citadel the Bowls Club (below left) is popular.

Badminton in Blackpool
The Badminton Club at Blackpool Citadel meets every Friday night.

Special abilities
In early October 2011, 'tweenagers' (right) in Yorkshire spent a weekend exploring the seven values of the Olympic and Paralympics Games and discovering how these could apply to their Christian faith. They also played three Paralympic sports, giving them an opportunity to explore new ways of making sport inclusive and discovering how God has given each of us special abilities.

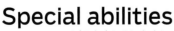

SMART sport in Staines

Sports Ministry and Recreational Time – SMART – is an exciting new programme which has been developed at Staines Corps in Middlesex to encourage the church and local community to come together. Football is a key element in the programme and the SA Stainash (Staines and Ashford Club) competes in the local Christian Football League. Recently the SA Stainash Vets team (right) was formed.

Looking ahead
Nurturing future generations

THE Salvation Army believes everyone is precious to God. In corps and centres across the territory, people of all ages are welcomed and encouraged to discover how much he loves them and the possibilities he has for their lives.

Parent-and-toddler groups reach hundreds of children, parents, grandparents and other carers every week. It's an opportunity for little ones to have lots of fun while the adults chat, share experiences and, sometimes, seek spiritual support.

Here's a selection of some of the activities that take place.

Charlotte is just one of the children at Stowmarket in Suffolk who enjoys coming to the parent-and-toddler group....it's so popular the corps now has two sessions.

Snacks

Healthy snack time at Bedlington parent-and-toddler group in Northumberland (left).

Fun in the sun

A mild October meant it was still warm enough to play outside in Doncaster.

'In God's name let us work as we never worked before for the little ones of the world'

William Booth

Everyone welcome

A great time at Kettering – and it's not just for mums and toddlers (below and right).

Little angels

There's fun for everyone at Winton in Bournemouth.

151

At Felixstowe, Amy gets a little help from Sunday school teacher Alicia.

Faith and fun

CHRISTIAN teaching is provided from an early age at activities such as Sunday schools, after-school clubs and holiday programmes. These are open to anyone. The Army's Territorial Children's Ministries Unit provides excellent resources for leaders, while the Schools and Colleges Unit produces material for schools.

In conjunction with the Religious Education curriculum, many corps run Ultimate Church Visits where children spend a day at The Salvation Army learning more about the organisation.

Holiday club fun at Cwmbran, South Wales.

After-school club in Southsea.

Bedlington

Bedlington Youth Club celebrated Harvest with a 'best pumpkins' competition – a bit messy but great fun.

Southwark craft day

There was lots of noise, dressmaking, drumming and laughter during a holiday club at Southwark in south London. The corps, which has a multicultural congregation, celebrated Black History Month in October 2011.

A spiritual future

Exploring faith

House groups

Glenda Dixon's house group (above) is one of eight held regularly for members and friends of Birmingham Citadel.

Alpha

The Alpha course is for people who want to find out more about the Christian faith. At the Treehouse Community and Faith Centre at the University of Bedfordshire, students explore the meaning of Christianity, the meaning of life and enjoy a meal during the course run by Luton Corps (above right). At Staines Corps (right) the Alpha evening also starts with a light meal, followed by a presentation and discussions.

Midweek meeting

The Grizedale house group meets every other Wednesday at Blackpool Citadel. For some of the members this is their 'church' as they may be unable to attend on Sundays.

I N addition to attending Sunday worship, the Army encourages to people to take every opportunity to develop their spiritual lives and discover the possibilities that faith in Jesus offers.

Many centres run the internationally-recognised Alpha course, which explores the Christian faith. For those already on the journey there are development courses, Bible studies and prayer groups.

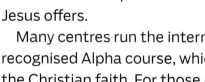

Bible study and prayer

At Leicester South a group meets once a week to study the Bible and pray.

Final reflections

I N 1878 Salvation Army co-founder Catherine Booth presented the first flag to Coventry Corps, and today the Army flag is displayed in most Army halls.

One morning in October 2011 David Heath, an adherent member at Chelmsford Corps in Essex, noticed a striking reflection of the top of the flag onto the wooden wall behind it. With its distinctive red, blue and yellow – representing the blood of Jesus Christ, the purity of God and the fire of the Holy Spirit – the flag is topped by an 'S' and a cross. This emphasises the Army's belief that everyone can be saved from sin through faith in Jesus Christ. The possibility of peace with God is available to all.

Love for God and people motivated William and Catherine Booth. This remains the reason behind everything the 21st-century Salvation Army is and does.

'While there remains one dark soul without the light of God, I'll fight'

William Booth

Index